GREEN BANANAS

TINA HOLT

Quantity sales special discounts are available on quantity purchases by corporations, associations, and others. For details, contact the publisher at the address above.

Orders by U.S. trade bookstores and wholesalers. Email info@BeyondPublishing.net

The Beyond Publishing Speakers Bureau can bring authors to your live event. For more information or to book an event contact the Beyond Publishing Speakers Bureau speak@BeyondPublishing.net

The Author can be reached directly at BeyondPublishing.net

Manufactured and printed in the United States of America distributed globally by BeyondPublishing.net

BEYOND
PUBLISHING

New York | Los Angeles | London | Sydney

ISBN Hardcover: 978-1-952884-98-6

DEDICATION

To my late father, who dedicated his life to loving, uplifting, and encouraging others.

To my late mother, who was the strongest woman I ever knew and inspires me to this day.

To my three incredible sons—Travis, Joshua, and Cory Holt. Thank you for allowing me to give and receive a level of love I never knew existed.

To my grandchildren, who bring me such joy.

I love you all.

PROLOGUE

The Eternal Value of Quality Time

There will come a time in our lives when we will look back on our most curious human adventure.

There will be joys, pains, successes, and failures—some fun things and some sadnesses.

For many of us, what will arise from the journey will be our greatest life treasures. We will recall the moments spent with people we love most— parents, children, grandchildren, special friends— and we will know that nothing else in our life measured up to the value of those moments.

You and I are living real time in those moments. The times we will one day fondly recall are the moments we are living today.

Let's agree to determine to make these precious moments a priority in our lives every day. The thinking and strategies in *Green Bananas* only make sense when your heart is full of the things you love most.

We only live our life once. If we live it right, once is enough.

Tina Holt
August 2020

ONE

We Are All Green Bananas

"Tina, please start buying green bananas."

What a strange statement. But truer, more needful words were never spoken. You see, after my first cancer diagnosis, my automatic response to any invitation to a long-term goal or activity was, "Are you kidding? I don't even buy green bananas!"

But my friend's words were all I had to hear to know what I needed to do. It was time to change the way I thought.

At the time, I believed I was a superwoman. I had pulled it off. I had it all: a successful real estate career, a loving husband, three wonderful sons—all of whom were active in sports, music, and such—a nice home, and a nice car. I was living the good life, just as I had planned. Or was I?

Then, it happened.

I discovered a lump in my breast. I was 37 years old with a young family—a family that needed me. The possibility of cancer was one thing I had never wanted to face. I did not have time for it.

But I did the right thing and went to the doctor and had a

biopsy. Then, I went about my business as best as I could. A couple of days later, my doctor called and said, "Tina are you sitting down?"

I said, "No, but I have a feeling I need to."

"You have breast cancer," she said.

The first thing I thought was, *I don't have time for this.* My life was busy, and I didn't have any room on my calendar for cancer. How was I going to fit doctor appointments and treatments and surgery into my life? I was so busy raising my sons, working, keeping my home, serving on local real estate committees, and maintaining social relationships. There were no sensible options—except that I would somehow have to make time for treatment while living my life, versus making time for my life during treatment.

There was a huge distinction in that for me. I wasn't about to give up anything in my life. I would not give in to this tiger. Cancer was going to be a tight squeeze, but I would make it work—even though I was so busy living my life in the here and now, I didn't even know what I was going to have for dinner the next day. Cancer was definitely going to be a gamechanger.

But I was determined to make it work—to make it all work.

Like other major events or illnesses, life completely changes after a cancer diagnosis, when you are literally fighting for your life. It changes your perspective. Your thinking changes. My head felt crowded. It was like having a noise in the background that never went away. It's incredibly sobering to watch the spring or summer flowers bloom and think, *Wow, I wonder if I'll ever see that again?* This is when you really start to pay attention to the fact that life is a privilege and a gift that we too often take for granted. My mortality had never been a part of my life before.

It was like having a noise in the background that never went away. It's incredibly sobering to watch the spring or summer flowers bloom and think, *Wow, I wonder if I'll ever see that again?*

I began to make some changes that reflected my new-found perspective. Thinking back, some of the changes seem more automatic than anything. I needed to be in control of my life. I went through the house, getting rid of as much of my everyday stuff as I could by donating or selling the things. I remember climbing into the attic and searching the linen closet and bringing out all the good stuff we never used, the stuff we were saving for a "special occasion". Well, cancer was certainly a special occasion. It was time to use it.

In fact, it was then that I realized that every day— even my pre-cancer days— were all special occasions.

Every morning, when each of us wake up with the ability to walk, talk, and make decisions, it is another day of opportunity. It is also true that so many of us wake up in pain—whether it is physical pain or emotional pain—something that hurts, a wound or a loss that creates a hurt we carry with us. Most of us keep it all hidden away from the people around us. But the new day is still given to us. What we do with that day is up to us. We can waste it catching up on family, friends, or work "drama", or we can make best use of the day with developing ourselves and helping others do the same. As much as we are able, we should have an idea every morning as to what we plan to do that day to move ourselves towards our dreams and goals—towards the only life we have been given.

Dreams and Goals

I also started to think about my interior life, and what I wanted it to be about.

I had moved to the mountains ten years prior, but I missed the coast. I had always loved real estate, but felt it might be time to stretch myself. I knew there were others who might find answers in my journey, and my gifts had proven I was able to influence the thinking of others. I decided to invest significantly in myself and my relationships with my friends, but I needed to determine who was or was not reciprocating. I knew my personal faith was beginning to suffer, because I was using "busy" as a reason to not keep my spiritual tank full.

I could not escape the big question: "Tina, what do you really want in life?" If I had a magic wand, what would my life look like? Where would I want to live? Do I want a want a different career? Am I content with my relationships? My faith? My journey became my life. I would never be satisfied again. I did NOT have it all. I wanted more. I began a life-long, soul-searching journey when I received my first cancer diagnosis.

I could not escape the big question: "Tina, what do you really want in life?" If I had a magic wand, what would my life look like?

What city or state would you like to live in? What style of house would you live in? What would the interior of your house look like? What qualities would you want in a spouse or significant other? How many children would you have? What would your career of choice be? How much money would you earn? What would your wardrobe look like? What kind of car or truck would you drive?

Once you discover these desires, take a quiet moment to close your eyes and imagine it as if it were so. Get that feeling down in your gut—that same feeling you get when you know you are going on vacation or buying that new car—and you "feel" excited while imagining what you are going to do when you get there! I would encourage you to even create a vision board, or at the very least, keep a visible list of these things you can refer to daily, perhaps on your desktop or on the fridge.

You can absolutely have the life you always dreamed about.

As a real estate professional and a life and leadership coach, my job has always been to develop agents and others—people from many professions and walks of life—to become the best they can possibly be in their careers and in their purposes in life. I am good at it and have guided many people to lives they now love.

One of the techniques I use in our conversations is to encourage the agents to ask themselves the magic-wand question. I help agents zero in on what is important to them and where they want their career and their personal lives to be in two years, or five, or fifteen. Then, we discuss whatever strategies we need to implement in order to be successful. It becomes about setting goals and working toward achieving those goals. It is surprising how many of the things that matter to you are within reach, if you stick your head up out of the water.

I heavily invest in my personal and professional relationships. I have learned, firsthand, the truth in Zig Ziglar's quote, "You can have everything in life you want, if you will help enough other people get what they want."

Toward that end, I also encourage sales agents to ask this question of their clients and the people around them. If you are working on a real estate transaction, it really helps them to hone in on exactly what kind of property they are looking for, what they need in a home or office space, what they can truly afford, and even what might happen a few years down the road.

I have learned firsthand the truth in Zig Ziglar's quote, "You can have everything in life you want, if you will help enough other people get what they want."

Over the next several chapters, I am going to outline some ideas and principles that will help you achieve the life you dream about.

It all begins with admitting that you are a Green Banana.

That's correct. You heard me right. A Green Banana.

What, exactly, does that mean?

It wasn't until I was going along, thinking I had beaten cancer after 14 years of being in the clear and building my career—when BAM! I was hit with a second cancer diagnosis.

I was so busy living in the moment, getting ahead, furthering my career, that I stopped enjoying the everyday, the special moments life has to offer. The catalyst for this change of mindset came when I was talking to a friend. I was completely satisfied with getting stuff done, developing others' lives, and scurrying from one appointment, one meeting, one conference call, to another—that life had become a blur. I imagine my busyness was because I had the big C-word hanging over my head. I could not slow down. I was a bullet train that wasn't making any stops. I scoffed whenever anyone mentioned a long-term plan or commitment.

After finishing a lunch date the day before I was to begin my second round of chemo treatments, my friend said, "Tina, please start buying green bananas."

Talk about a lightning bolt from heaven. It was that very moment that it hit me. While I had always believed it was important to live in the moment, to be fully present wherever you are, in whatever you are doing, I was missing one component of the happy, successful life. I had to reclaim my own power to dream again.

I needed to recapture the wisdom and necessity of planning for the future for my own life, of setting things in motion that would help create the magic-wand life of tomorrow.

I was missing one component of the happy, successful life. I had to reclaim my own power to dream again.

I stopped living just for today and quite a bit of the noise my cancer had created. I went out and bought a bunch of the greenest bananas I could find and set them on my counter as a reminder. Because that was the point of the magic-wand life of tomorrow. I needed to start planning for more than just today. I had to start planning out the rest of my life. In order to enjoy the green bananas, I had to put them aside and have a little patience and wait for them to ripen over the next few days.

My goal in writing this book is not to drop a bunch of candy bombs on you and walk away. I don't want to give you a bunch of hollow platitudes about how to live your best life. I want you to have more. Many of us plugged into the sacred reality of our journey have come to understand that we have been given a gift to live our lives with a higher sense of understanding and peace. I believe we can all live a more abundant life and yes, buying green bananas is part of the abundant life.

WE ARE ALL GREEN BANANAS

As I said, I didn't want to just give you a bunch of feel good quotes—although, I love good quotes and affirmations—nor do I want to give you a list of dos and don'ts. I decided to write a story, a parable, to illustrate what I mean about the joy and awareness of the green banana. That's right—the awareness of the green banana.

We learn best through stories. The power of teaching through a story is what made Jesus the most influential teacher who ever walked the earth. His parables are still discussed and mined for wisdom, even to this day. We remember stories and characters, and we understand meaning more readily through story than dry lectures. We are wired for stories—they stick.

I want you to understand the joy and challenge of the green banana. It is my modern-day parable and gift for you. We all need to ripen into the people we want to be to live the life we want for ourselves and our families. It's going to take work and commitment. Life is hard work. Achieving your goals and dreams takes determination and perseverance. Just remember, whenever you are tempted to quit, it's alright to say, "Hey, I'm a green banana. I am still in the ripening process. And that's okay."

It's okay to rest. It's okay to take a break.

It's not okay to quit on yourself!

TWO

Have you ever noticed that when you are driving, your car goes where your eyes go? That's why it's important to keep your eyes focused on the road ahead. Life is like that, in a sense: your life follows your thoughts. Be aware of which thoughts you entertain.

I've come to understand that a lot of people aren't positive by nature. It's not their gift.

There are days and times I struggle, like everyone else. That is why I find it most important to start each day with something positive. The first thing I do when I wake up is thank God for another day—another day to explore possibilities and opportunities to achieve my dreams, to love and spend time with those I care about, to be the best leader, speaker, coach, mentor, mom, Mimi, and friend I can be.

How do you start your day?

Awareness

I recommend starting your day with asking yourself: "How do I feel: low, so-so, fine, good, or great? Why do I feel this way?" This is usually determined by something you are currently dealing with in life or must deal with today, whether good or bad. For many of us, it is waiting for us when we wake up in the morning. The next question is: "What could I do to feel better?" Maybe that answer would be something like exercise, lose weight, change careers, find new friends, end a toxic relationship, etc. The answers for many seem impossible.

Keep a journal and write your answers down. You will have to decide to make the changes necessary to get yourself healthy and achieve your goals.

Desires

What do you want for your life? You have to know what it is you want before you can create a plan to make it happen. I find planning is difficult for many people. I am often surprised when I am talking with people who have no idea what they want. Most just want to make it through the day, the week, the month, or as long as they can simply survive. What are you thinking? Your answer could be a big indication that you are on a dead-end path. If that is the case, it's okay. It's not the end of the world. That's why you and I are having this conversation.

A great start to changing that mindset is reading this book. It all starts with how you think. This is where it all begins, and the most critical element of your success in living the best version of yourself and the life you wish to design for yourself. Start with a mindset makeover.

Give yourself a check-up from the neck up! Get rid of that stinking thinking. When you can't be happy about where you are in life, be happy about where you are not. When you have limitations, focus on what you *can* do, not what you cannot do. Those thoughts come, but you don't have to entertain them. I have found that on the days I feel a little low, nothing brings me to a positive place faster than doing something for someone else. Some may think, "If I am feeling low, why would I want to get around someone else and possibly bring them down?" That is the perfect time to go be a blessing to someone else. I didn't say bring them down. Go be a blessing!

Believe it or not, there are people praying for what you currently have, and that could be something as simple as your next meal. I want to encourage you to spend some time being thankful for your current circumstances, even if they may not feel optimal for you at the moment.

Give yourself a check-up from the neck up!

Get rid of that stinking thinking.

When you can't be happy about where you are in life,

be happy about where you are not.

Be Grateful

It's easy to focus on the negative parts of life, especially when you might be going through a difficult time. But throughout my cancer journey, I learned that dwelling on the bad only made things worse. Instead, ask yourself what is right in your life, and change your focus to those things.

There were days when I didn't want to get out of bed. I felt trapped. I struggled at times. I physically hurt. My head pounded, and I had pain like I had never had before. I no longer recognized the person in the mirror, and I would get discouraged. But I would make myself go to work and live life as normally as possible. It made my life matter. I was grateful for the opportunity to continue earning a living, as the bills didn't stop coming just because I was battling cancer.

I had always wanted to buy and sell—or flip—an investment property. I bought and sold my first one while going through treatment. It was crazy. I did something I had always wanted to do in a moment when I seemed to be at my weakest. I was able to do the painting and several other things, which saved money and increased profit. Although it was difficult, I chose to focus on the things I "could do", rather than the things I couldn't. There would be no excuses for me. I would not have it.

Faith

For many, faith plays an important part in their life journey. I know it does for me. The sacred part of ourselves needs to come to the front if we are to grow and get larger in achieving our dreams. Prayer and meditation are vital gateways in taking control of your life.

There will be moments when our sacred intuition will be the only thing that makes sense. It must be cultivated and nourished. I look for sacred conversations wherever I can find them. They are so important to my soul and my larger perspective of life. I am always surprised how enthusiastic others are to have meaning-of-life conversations. Asking others thoughtful questions is one of my favorite pastimes and empowering to the development of my own thinking.

Life circumstances and the challenges that come with them are quite different when managed through a sacred lens.

The sacred part of ourselves needs to come to the front if we are to grow and get larger in achieving our dreams.

GPS

I'm fascinated by my phone's navigation system. Remember unfolding maps in the car? If you are younger, you have no idea what we went through. The maps were folded like small accordions, and when unfolded, were the size of the kitchen table. They were printed on both sides, and it was horrible to just find where you were on the map, much less figure out where you wanted to go.

What a chore that was, and so confusing. But now, we have this amazing GPS technology. Just set it and let it tell you how to get where you want to go. However, many of you still second-guess it, argue with it, and make your own decisions, sometimes turning it off and going your own way. And then, there is that little finish flag marking the end of the trip. Seeing that flag gives me the confidence to keep moving as the distance closes in.

Our GPS systems are terrific life lessons. Just like I can see the little finish flag marking my location on the screen, it's prudent to look out ahead and see your life or career path goal. It's out there for sure. It might seem far away, but it is hugely motivating to know the finish flag is there. Keep your eyes on it and keep moving.

Imagine what it is going to feel like when you finally arrive. Free? Elated? Satisfied? Excited? Maybe a whole bunch of green banana feelings. If you are struggling with feelings, just remember what it feels like to go on vacation. Yep, achieving your goals is like that—quite refreshing and exciting.

Take a moment and imagine yourself in that place. How does it feel?

Kindness

Mark Twain said, "Kindness is a language the deaf can hear and the blind can see." A simple act of kindness can do more to brighten a person's day than you might realize. Hold the door for the person whose arms are full of packages or kids. Allow someone else to take your seat on the bus or place in line. Call that person you've promised to call but are always too busy. Help the obviously destitute person pay for their groceries. These small acts of kindness are powerful and go a long way in not only helping another person through a difficult time, but also in helping yourself. Being kind makes you feel good. And, if you feel good, you can tap into your power more than when you are only thinking of yourself and your troubles. Break away from the tyranny of self-doubt, sadness, and discouragement, and perform a random act of kindness. You'll be surprised at how good it makes you feel.

Small acts of kindness are powerful and go a long way in not only helping another person through a difficult time, but also helping yourself. Being kind makes you feel good.

Intentionality

This book is about deciding you are a green banana and putting strategies in place to help you ripen into the person you want to become. One surefire strategy to keep you on the road is to do what you say you are going to do. If you have decided that starting school or going back to school is what you want to do, and you want to investigate schools—don't fret about it—do it. And don't make excuses. You can have excuses or results. You can't have both!

One technique I suggest to clients is that they make an intentional plan for each day and then stick to it. Before you go to bed at night, know what you plan to accomplish tomorrow. Granted, tomorrow may bring things you don't expect. That's okay. Chances are you can accomplish the goals you set and conquer the unexpected. But, even if you can't cross off everything on your list, be kind to yourself. Focus on the things you *were* able to do, and celebrate your progress. Making a plan and sticking with it will help keep you focused, energized, and organized. Being kind to yourself will help you remember your own self-love and self-worth.

Good intentions don't get you anywhere—good actions do!

As my friend and mentor, John Maxwell, says, all you need to do to be intentional is to start.

Promises, Promises

I think everyone knows what it feels like to be on the receiving end of a broken promise. It hurts. It's rude. It unsettling and makes it difficult to trust. You need to determine to keep your promises, no matter how small. We all are only as good as our word. But we are also only human, and there will be days when we fall short. And that's okay. Just don't allow one or two setbacks to become an everlasting gobstopper of excuses to continue to fall short. Be sure to get back on track tomorrow.

Many people have good intentions, but unfortunately, without action. To maintain integrity, it is important to do what we say we will, when we say we will. We all know life happens, and there are times legitimate things keep us from fulfilling a promise.

We all are only as good as our word.

When my youngest son and his family were stationed in South Korea, I promised them I would visit once during his two-year tour. When they first moved there, I was still recovering from cancer treatments and major surgery, so I thought it best to wait a year. As they were approaching their second year there, I learned that mold is quite an issue in South Korea, which created two other areas of concern for me. Because I have no lymph nodes in my right arm, I have to wear a compression sleeve while traveling; it isn't pleasant, and it is an extremely long flight—not to mention, flying causes swelling for me. Just a trip to the west coast is pushing it for me.

The second reason, one of the chemo medicines I was on really takes a toll on your lungs, and mold freaks me out! You see, I love adventure, and I love my children and grandchildren more than anything. I wanted to experience South Korea, and I so badly wanted to see my son and his precious family, but I had legitimate concerns to not make the trip. That experience made me feel so bad. I never intended to let them down, as they were wanting me to come as badly as I wanted to go. But here's the deal: they know I love them with all my heart. I had to make the best decision for *me* at the time.

There will be times when you will need to go back on a promise. Just be sure to communicate your reasons for doing so, and people will usually understand.

Practice Self-Care

Any of us who have ever flown in an airplane know the drill when the flight attendant instructs passengers to put their own oxygen mask on before helping others. I know it's an analogy that has been used over and over, but it's so brilliant and true, it bears repeating: take care of yourself first! You are no good to anyone else if you can't breathe. If we extend this metaphor out to daily life on the ground, the premise is still the same. Take care of yourself before taking care of someone else. It's essential.

You are no good to anyone else if you can't breathe.

What does self-care look like? It can be as simple as keeping up with your yoga classes, taking a long walk by yourself, reading a book, getting massages—whether it's just you or a couples massage with your spouse or significant other—or taking weekend getaways. Or self-care can be a little more intense, like setting healthy boundaries and learning to say "no". This is especially true for those of you with people-pleasing desires. I struggled with that for many years, and I still have to work hard at keeping myself in check. For some, the best self-care could be simply unplugging for a certain number of hours or days. For others, it could be indulging in a special treat or going dancing. But you should always be doing something that makes *you* happy.

Environmental Controls

It's become easy enough to control the temperature of a room. Too hot—turn up the AC. Too cold—turn up the heat or wrap another blanket around your shoulders.

But your environment is more than just the place you call home. Your environment is also the people in your life, who share your workspace or your social activities. You should always choose a circle of friends who will support your dreams and cheer you on from the sidelines. It's not a good idea to live in an environment with toxic and emotionally draining people.

Disengage from these negative people. We all know someone who, if you ask how they are doing, is going to tell you everything that has been wrong for the past 10 years, or maybe their entire life. I'm not saying we shouldn't care about those people; I'm just saying don't engage when you know that is the response you will get. They will always find a problem for every solution. Encourage them, pray for them, and help them when they are in need, but don't allow them to drag you down. This might mean cutting off some relationships— maybe just for a while—but still, the hard work of reaching your goals might require leaving some people out of your inner circle.

It is impossible for you to be a dumping station for everyone else's garbage and stay on track to obtaining your personal and professional dreams. Don't misunderstand my point here: it's always okay to have a listening ear to those in need, but avoid being that listening ear for those who consistently create their own problems and expect you to be the ear that listens.

When I battled cancer the first time, I had to distance myself from someone who was very dear to me, because she is an extreme worrier and was always focused on what was wrong or could go wrong. I knew I couldn't fight the fight to stay alive and overcome that horrid disease if I was allowing her garbage to fill me. Setting healthy boundaries falls under both the self-care and environmental control categories.

It is impossible for you to be a dumping station for everyone else's garbage and stay on track to obtaining your personal and professional dreams.

It is equally as important to live in an environment where you have positive, successful, uplifting people. Seek out relationships that make you feel good and will move you closer to your dreams.

Remember our all-important question: if you had a magic wand and could create the life you want, what would it look like?

THREE

After my first cancer diagnosis, I got rid of all the old kitchenware and linens and brought out the good stuff.

I want people to understand that although it is important to plan for the future, it is also important to enjoy what you have—here and now. You, your family, and your friends are worthy of the good stuff. They are worthy of your best. And I'm not just talking about stuff. You, your family, and your friends are worthy of the best possible you. Show them the best parts of you. Even if you don't feel like it sometimes.

Most of us in the working world invest in our hair, nails, wardrobe—everything to make us *look* good. But many times, our outsides don't match our insides. And that's not necessarily a bad thing. Like I said, we are all green bananas. We are all growing and changing. But what I want you to take to heart is that when you look good, you *feel* good. I want you to feel as good on the inside as you look on the outside. That's why I want you to envision the life you want.

It is an important part of our life adventure that we try to be the best versions of ourselves every day.

Ladies, you know the way you carry yourself when you are dressed to the nines is much different than when you are in lounging or some other casual clothes. Guys, you also carry yourself different when you are dressed in a nice suit.

Someone once said, "Dress for the job you want, not the job you have." There is a lot of wisdom in that little statement.

It is very important that we try to be the best version of ourselves every day.

The Best Way to Predict Your Future Is to Plan for It

After my first diagnosis, there were a few times when I seriously wondered if I was going to make it. It is quite a lonely space. You question everything and see yourself in a way that you have never seen yourself before. It's hard to think straight or even know exactly what to think.

However, I knew every time I looked at my children, I understood the only thing that mattered. I simply had to make it! A life without their mother was not an option for me. I didn't want anyone else to raise my boys. No one else could love them or understand them like I do.

Yet, I knew that some things were out of my control. Having cancer made me wonder about what I would do if I only had a year or a few months to live. What might be hiding around the corner, waiting to jump out and rearrange my life all over again? It seemed that maybe I didn't have as much control of my future as I once had, or I thought I had.

I set my mind on other things. My diagnosis gave me the permission to figure out what I really cared about, what I really wanted to do, and most importantly, it taught me to be intentional about getting what I desired for me and my family.

That, to me, is the key to getting to the place you visualized with your magic wand.

The first step is to identify what you want in life, and the second is to recognize the obstacles that might be holding you back from achieving your goals and find ways to hurdle those obstacles.

My diagnosis gave me the permission to figure out what I really cared about, what I really wanted to do, and most importantly, it taught me to be intentional about getting what I desired for me and my family.

This is not always easy. Some might be suffocating in a toxic relationship that is difficult to end. But I just want to encourage you that you do not have to stay in an unhealthy relationship. Your first priority should always be yourself, and if your needs are not met, you have no obligation to stay. It is also important to plan your way of escape and be intentional about the choices you make to get to a place where you can begin to realize your goals. In circumstances such as these, find a confidant or friend for wisdom.

Oftentimes, our biggest obstacle is our own mindset, and is usually a result of past or present pain, unforgiveness of ourselves or others, failures, or hanging on to past mistakes when what we really need to do is examine these things, own them, and learn from them.

Sadly, some of your own family or friends may not want you to be successful. It's hard to hear. They are not always our greatest champions. For some, they are afraid you will outgrow them; others may be afraid that your success will make them look bad. As a result, you need to understand that while these people may love you—and you may love them—they are not going to support you as you grow or cheer you on as you become more and more successful. That doesn't mean you should stop loving them; you just need to know what to expect or not expect.

Sometimes, the obstacle seems to be a lack of culturally accepted education. If so, plan to go back to school. If your goal is a new car, then make the appropriate choices that will get you that new car or house. Rather than thinking of all the reasons you can't, simply start thinking about ways you *can.*

Sometimes, it is a matter of just doing it. You have to get out of your own way and stop the stinkin' thinkin' that's holding you back.

Excuses or results.
You can't have both.

We have more control over certain areas of our lives and circumstances than we think. As I said earlier, getting a cancer diagnosis changes your perspective. If we all knew we only had a year left on Earth, we would all get really, really busy. This is how you should live now. Don't misunderstand me, I don't mean this to be depressing in that you should live in fear of dying. Actually, quite the opposite: you should live in fear of *not* living your best life. My intent is that you get busy *living!*

Identify what is keeping you from having the life you want. Oftentimes, it's *you.* You are keeping yourself down. Stop the excuses of "life just seems to get in the way", "once I pay off my student loans, I'll make some big changes", "once I have a baby", "once my children are grown…" The list could go on and on. You know your self-talk. Examine it, and hurdle the obstacles.

Forgiveness vs. Unforgiveness

If you are living with resentment in your heart, I can assure you, it will hold you back. Unforgiveness is like drinking poison and waiting for the other person to die. That's just not how it works.

Forgiveness will be, for many of us, the most important life lesson we will need to learn. I can assure you, the other person has moved on, while you are struggling to push your way through the day to day, exhausted due to the resentment you are carrying around daily. It's robbing you of energy and passion, whether you think so or not.

Some of the toughest things I've had to forgive and overcome are things for which I never received an apology. I forgave because I deserved to be free of the anger. I forgave because I deserved to be free of the hurt. I forgave because it took energy to hold on to all those things, and that was energy that deserved to be spent on something that could benefit *me*.

It's easier to let go than to harbor unnecessary emotions, but it takes practice. The more you do it, the easier it becomes, and the freer you will be. Perhaps it's *you* that you need to forgive the most.

I forgave because I deserved to be free of the anger. I forgave because I deserved to be free of the hurt. I forgave because it took energy to hold on to all those things, and that was energy that deserved to be spent on something that could benefit *me*.

Be intentional about knowing and getting what you need.

Begin each morning with your eyes set on the prize. Visualize your future self as though you have already arrived and keep moving forward. See yourself in the fast or luxury car, you and your family on that great vacation, with the career path or new position you wish to have. Look at that vision board or list you created. My vision board is simply pictures saved on my iPad screen where I can see them daily. As I achieve the goals, I delete and add new ones.

And by the way, this is also true for young people. Young adults think they have plenty of time to achieve their goals. Well, I'm here to tell you that time goes fast. Plan accordingly, and trust yourself.

Your intuition is important and, oftentimes, accurate. It's the go-with-your-gut mentality. If an idea for a new goal arises, jump on it. Paste it on your vision board, make it part of your overall plan. Just remember: it's alright if plans change. The important thing is you keep moving forward without fear.

As you accomplish goals,

always create new ones.

About That Fear

Get ready to swallow it up. FEAR stands for False-Evidence-Appearing-Real or Face-Everything-And-Rise, whichever speaks to your heart. Fear is the root of so many other issues. When it comes to overcoming fear, I turn to one of my favorite childhood verses: Psalms 56:3, "When I am afraid, I will trust in Thee."

Make the decision to eliminate fear and anxiety in your life. A good start is being aware of why you feel that way. Ask yourself, *Why do I feel this way, and what would make me feel better?* If fear is overwhelming, it might be prudent to seek out a counselor, coach, or minister.

I was afraid of my cancer diagnosis. My fear of what it meant froze me. Both times, my soul could have easily been destroyed. Today, when I have pain in any area for more than a couple of days, I can easily fall back into the trap of fear with thoughts such as, "Has the cancer returned and spread? If so, will I die? What will I have to go through? I don't want my family to see me suffer."

We can't necessarily control the thoughts that come, but again, we have total control over the thoughts we actually entertain. When those thoughts come, I instantly turn them into thoughts of, "I believe I am here for a purpose, and I know I still have work to do in helping others reach their highest potential and accomplish their dreams. I want to see my grandchildren grow into adults, marry, and have their own families. My life matters until my last breath."

Do Your Research

Any new endeavor requires a certain amount of research. If you want to purchase a new car, you research various models to find the one that best suits you and your needs. If you want to change your eating habits and lose weight—you might research and find what matches your lifestyle—preferably something that includes lots of cookies. No, just kidding! The point is research is a necessary part of making any big changes and good decisions.

Whether you are planning to add a child to your family, purchase a new home, get married, change your career, move up the ladder with your current employer, open your own business, go back to school—whatever you need to do to get started on the road to achieving your goals—requires knowledge with a sprinkle of understanding.

There are a couple of ways I prefer to gather knowledge. One is to find a mentor or coach—someone who can guide you down the path. The other is to tap into my people resources. Chances are, someone you know can help or they know someone who can. I have found that successful people truly love to share their knowledge with people they believe are serious about achieving their goals and finding their own level of success. Make friends with people who are already where you want to be. If you don't know them, someone you know likely does. Ask for an introduction.

When it comes to mentors and coaches, how do you know it's a good fit? Referrals are always best, perhaps someone you know has utilized those services. Maybe post a social media request to see who people recommend. A Google search and look at their profile to see what you may have in common. Look for reviews and testimonials.

Successful people truly love to share their knowledge with people they believe are serious about achieving their goals and finding their own level of success.

If your goal is to finish or start a degree, you will need to know which school to go to, how much it will cost, and what grants or scholarships or loans are available to someone in your particular situation. A good place to start is with the admissions counselor at your college of choice. They love to help students find a way into their schools.

There is nothing wrong with asking for help. Sometimes, it can be the best thing you can do. If need be, ask a friend to assist you while you sign up for online classes, or maybe ask a friend to meet you somewhere to celebrate your new chosen path right after you sign up for classes. Invite a friend to go to the car dealership with you. There is nothing wrong in having a cheerleader or two on the sidelines. We all need a support system of family, friends, neighbors, clergy, teachers, or mentors—people who will stand alongside when we need them. Know who your support circle is and keep it somewhat small, but strong.

Cheerleaders can come in more ways than friends. It would be wise to seek out a coach or counselor to help you make the decisions you need to make. A counselor can help you figure out why you haven't taken those first steps or resisted researching, or you may need a friend to offer that little nudge of encouragement. Perhaps you need that friend who's always willing to offer that swift kick you need.

I coach and develop successful real estate agents. I also coach people in leadership positions, other professions, and walks of life— including those going through chemotherapy. I help them become the best people they can be. I put the magic wand in their hand, so to speak, and ask them to visualize their goals and their life five years down the road. I encourage them to be wise with their time—for everything you say yes to, you must say no to something, as there are

but so many waking hours in the day and so much to do. Then, we

figure out the steps it takes to get where they wish to be.

I recently coached two ladies who reached out to me. One is

married to the other's ex, and there is a child involved who spends

time in both households. These women obviously want things to work

out best for the child and all involved. As you can imagine, this is

a delicate and challenging situation. Part of my advice was to focus

on what they wanted for their relationship in the future. Everything

new starts today. Know what the vision is, what can we do to have a

healthy relationship, rather than angst.

I asked them how they could support each other and the child

involved. I am incredibly proud to say they have implemented my

suggestions, and combined with their own hard work and dedication,

they set their previous feelings aside and truly focused on what it took

to make it work. These women have actually gone on a trip together!

Life is too short for dysfunction. Growing up with a mother

who battled alcoholism involved more dysfunction than I care to

recall. She was a wonderful person, but the disease robbed our mother-

daughter relationship of many things. Although she made up for much

of that later in life by being the very best MeMaw, the past cannot

be changed. It is true, though—what is ahead of us is so much more

important than what is behind us.

We've all heard the saying that the windshield is so much bigger than the rear-view mirror. That is a true statement, and I love that it's meant to encourage us to look at the big picture in front of us, rather than the little one behind us. That's not to say we shouldn't learn from our experiences. As Green Bananas, we all should learn from our past and remember we all have so much to be grateful for. But we should allow no time for dysfunction and criticism. I can assure you, negativity and dysfunction cost you more than you realize and are guaranteed to hold you back from your dreams.

Life is too short for dysfunction. What is ahead of us is so much more important than what is behind us.

I want people to be the best possible versions of themselves — even if it means I might have to lean a little hard. I know the value of planning and intention when it comes to achieving your goals.

Embracing Change

This is a friend and colleague's story in his own words. I asked him if I could share this story, because I think his is the embodiment of what it means to envision the life you want and then make the necessary changes to achieve it.

Colleague's Story

"'I embrace change' is the statement I had been telling myself for years. But every time change would come around, I wanted to hide from it. I would smile outwardly and pretend to embrace it, but inwardly, I cringed. It was all so overwhelming.

The truth was, I loved the serenity and stability it could bring—calm, quiet, predictable stability.

I first met Tina in 2013, when she came to work at the same firm. She had been hired to take over one of our branch offices and steady a rocky ship, tossing and turning in turbulent seas. The first thing I noticed about Tina was her calmness.

For the next four years, Tina and I were colleagues, working in different offices. We were friendly, but not close. Our paths crossed occasionally, typically at company functions.

In 2017, I found myself in another difficult and turbulent situation. My branch manager had suddenly left the company. We also lost several agents who moved on to different jobs. This was exactly the kind of change I loathed, yet I smiled through it. As much as I wanted to hide from it—I couldn't. Tina was brought on to steady another rocky ship. Part of her plan was me—ME! She asked if I would help her steady a floundering ship.

More change for me. Great.

I did not realize it at the time, but 2017 began a stretch of transformational change for me. And it included a change in how I viewed change, itself. Shortly after we teamed up, Tina began working on me. She and I are two very different people, but Tina recognized my strengths and my weaknesses. She immediately saw my reaction to change, even when that change was the most necessary and the most beneficial to all. At first, I begrudgingly went along with all of her suggestions and changes, pretending to be fine with it all, but Tina saw through that. She coached me on my responses to change, reminding me that change is inevitable, and it's how we respond and react to the change that determines the outcome.

Slowly, I began to change the way I thought and made decisions. I started paying closer attention to the changes that happened around me. I even started to initiate my own changes, so I could have more control of the results. I started seeing change as an opportunity for growth. Change became a tool for me to use and not a by-product of my stability-seeking.

In helping me discover the positive power of change, Tina taught me to be a change agent, both for myself and for those around me. In the few short years since Tina and I teamed up, the change in my life has been significant: I have lost over 50 pounds, more than doubled my sales, and have taken on new leadership roles in community organizations. Beyond that, I moved houses and moved office locations–all big changes I historically would have shied away from. I have embraced these changes and so many more.

In helping me discover the positive power of change, Tina taught me to be a change agent, both for myself and for those around me.

Change happens. It is our reaction to change that determines if the change has a positive or a negative impact. Since 2017, Tina and I have grown from mere work colleagues to true partners in the growth and development of the people we lead. Tina is my sounding board, my coach, my mentor, and my friend. She has helped me grow into the kind of person who says, 'I embrace change' and mean it."

Basically, what I did was build his trust in me by getting to know each other, asking questions and being as authentic and transparent as I could possibly be. Once he learned he could trust me, he gained confidence in the leadership decisions I made that required change. I encouraged him that we either have to coach people up in the business or coach them out. I decided to make the office 100-percent paperless. Even though he liked having filing cabinets, he went along when I called the corporate office to come and take the filing cabinets away.

My coaching was about showing him that if we continued doing things the way they've always been done, we were going to continue getting the same results, and those results were not satisfactory to either of us. We were either growing or dying on the vine.

Early on in our relationship, we discussed the goals for the offices, and then, we made a plan that would enable us to meet those goals. Naturally, the plan included much-needed change. We discussed what things look like now, what the change will look like, as well as what the end game would look like. I used the RAMS technique .

Our relationship was key toward his success. We talked to each other, listened, and most importantly, set attainable goals for the offices.

Asking for Guidance

What does it mean to work hard and wise?

Working hard means you have to be diligent and intentional. You have to get up every day with the big picture in mind, and then, by default, you will make decisions that day that move you closer to your goal. For example, if I hang my swimsuit somewhere I have to see it daily with the intention of wearing it to the beach or pool, chances are I am going to make good decisions about what I eat that day and how much I move, and I'll be more aware of how I want to look when I *do* wear it. If that swimsuit is out of sight, it is going to be out of mind. This is why I mentioned the vision board or list in chapter two. It really is a great tool to keep you focused on your goals.

We only have so many hours in a day to take steps towards our goal as much of our time is dedicated to working in our current position, time with our spouse or significant other, family, social engagements, children's sports, etc. It is important that you are intentional about what you plan to accomplish every day. Again, I suggest having a prepared list every night before you go to bed of what you expect to accomplish the next day that will move you closer to your goals. If you want to change careers, then make a connection with someone already in that career, find a way to meet with or speak with that person. It might be a good idea to invite them to lunch or dinner. Ask them what they love most about their careers. Ask them what they dislike the most. Ask anything you wish to know about it. You will be pleasantly surprised that most people are willing to share. Smart people ask for advice.

Maybe you want to connect with two or three people in that field, so you can get different perspectives. Try to avoid the Negative Nancy or Ned talk. You know, the ones who have a problem for every solution. You will run into them from time to time, so simply move on and find another connection.

Even when you are doing well, I recommend always having a good mentor or coach. As you achieve your goals, there should always be a next-level dream, along with someone helping you to get there. I've had the pleasure of working with some very successful real estate agents over the years. Even those who are super-successful continue to reach out for coaching. You see, even though they are disciplined, driven, and willing to "do the work", having good support always helps you reach that next level. Yes, even successful people need support.

Even when you are doing well, I recommend always having a good mentor or coach. As you achieve your goals, there should always be a next-level dream, along with someone helping you to get there.

During a business planning and coaching session with a top-producing agent at the end of 2018, we were discussing her goals for 2019 and how I could support her. She had done a tremendous amount of business in 2018 without an assistant. When she shared her 2019 production goal of an increase of no less than five-million dollars in sales volume over—above the previous year of 20-million dollars in volume—I had no doubt she would achieve that goal, but I felt it best that she consider hiring an assistant. Needless to say, she reached her increased goal of over 25-million dollars in sales volume without an assistant. She was willing to "do the work". She frequently tracked her goals and stayed focused on the bigger picture.

You are likely wondering why I keep highlighting "do the work". To fulfill your purpose in life and become the person you were designed to be, you must be willing to "do the work". Otherwise, you will have to settle for what happens by default.

Do not compare yourself to others. You were designed to be you. You should only desire to be the best version of yourself, rather than "like" someone else. The world needs YOU, not carbon copies of others. Your only competition is the person in the mirror.

Many people have dreams and aspirations, but without "doing the work", it's simply a dream.

When it comes to setting goals for what you would like to achieve and/or who you wish to become, ask yourself: what are you willing to work for?

Set written goals. Your goals should be **RAMS**:

Relevant- To your chosen profession, personal goals, and values.

Attainable- Know what you most desire, as you will find a way to make it happen.

Measurable- Measure your progress, as this will serve as motivation to continue.

Specific- Your goal should be clear and include a due date.

FOUR

We Are Just Wired That Way

You were designed with a purpose and to have dreams and goals. It might not always feel that way, but believe me, you were born for a reason.

Whenever I speak with folks, I am always asked, "How do I know what my purpose is?"

Great question, and I have a great answer. Your purpose is what you are passionate about.

Ask yourself what is it that you enjoy doing so much that you would do for free if you had to. My passion has always been to help people reach their highest potential. I am passionate about problem-solving and helping people get where they want or need to be, to that place they envisioned when they waved the magic wand.

Once you figure out and claim your passion, the next thing to do is figure out how you can get paid for doing what you love.

And this is where all the other principles we discussed come into play.

Once you figure out what your passion is, you can begin to plan and be intentional about reaching your goal.

Once you figure out your passion, you can eliminate the obstacles.

Once you figure out your passion, you can do your research.

Once you figure out your passion, you can seek out mentors, counselors, or friends to help you along the way.

Once you figure out your passion, you can hand-select your support team. There are a few family members and friends you know will encourage you and cheer for you.

Ask yourself this question: **What is my strength zone?**

Your strength zone is your God-Given Talent (GGT). We all have *at least* one. I think the influences around us—especially social media—make us all too aware of our weaknesses or what we are not so good at, where we struggle. My advice is simple: get over what you don't do; get over your failures, which are often defined by doing something you aren't very good at. Focus on your strengths, your GGT, and operate from and within that zone. When you work from within your areas of strength, weak areas also grow.

Get over your failures, often defined by doing something you aren't very good at.

Focus on your strengths.

I think I've had this passion for helping people since I was five years old. It has always been what brings me the greatest joy. After both of my cancer diagnoses, this passion intensified. Each diagnosis offered me a whole new ability to help a whole new audience. It helped me to really help people zero in on what was holding them back and live as though they only had a year left on earth. It is the best way to live. The sense of urgency brings a fire to our daily living—that I can personally attest.

Every opportunity I get to speak on stage ignites my passion just as much as it does the audience. It thrills me to encourage and support others who are either stuck or just getting on track to accomplish their goals. Some may have gotten off track, and that's okay; I help them get right back on!

We've all heard the phrase, "added value". When I'm speaking and coaching, my goal is to simply add value by helping others figure out their GGT, help them see that forgiveness is possible, and help them understand they can have the life they envision.

I met an incredible young lady a couple years ago. She hadn't lived in the area too long and was having a difficult time finding her footing. She was a hard worker, kind and caring, but things just kept going wrong for her for one reason or another. I remember talking with her one particular day after learning her car had broken down, yet

again. She was in tears, because she didn't have the money for repairs.
The car had become a money pit, and in reality, she needed a new car.
I encouraged her to focus on finding ways she could buy another car,
rather than how she couldn't afford another repair.

Just a couple weeks later, she came to work in a new used car!
Over time, as we got to know each other, she would share her desires
in life, and I just kept encouraging her and offering suggestions. This
young lady has been unstoppable ever since. You see, with that first,
big step came confidence. Since that time, I am delighted to share she
has met weight loss, fitness, and home ownership goals, and most
recently, she bought a brand-new car. She was willing to do the work,
and it's truly amazing to watch!

Your Environment is Important

At one point, earlier in my marriage, I decided I wanted a
better school environment for our children. So, we packed up the
house, the kids, the dog, and the bird, and we moved four hours away
to the mountains of southwest Virginia. Several years later, and after
my first cancer diagnosis, I realized I missed the beach. And yes, we
moved back. We just didn't move back as a family unit. We figured out
a plan best for the children and made it work. I knew I needed to be in
a place that was conducive to my passion and my outlook. I needed to
be in a place that made me feel good. A place that would allow me to

be my best self, best mother, best leader, best daughter, and best friend.

But be aware! There is truth to that old chestnut, "The grass is always greener on the other side of the fence." It is greener where you water it. If you are considering a move, do your research to ensure *you* make the best move possible. Then again, we sometimes learn much more by making mistakes. I know I did. My move was no mistake, but I've made my share.

That might seem crazy to some, but I am fully committed to making the tough decisions necessary for my growth. I hope you will do the same.

I want to encourage you to be intentional with your life. Don't just let it pass by or wait until you are at the end of your life and faced with all of the "should have", "could have", "would have", thoughts. Whether you are young, old, or somewhere in between, your clock is ticking. Don't sit on the sidelines—get in the game! Figure out your passion, and then, figure out how to make it work for you. Get rid of the obstacles keeping you back, and plan for the future.

Remember that unexpected events and change will come, and usually when you least expect it. Be flexible and adaptable—willing to pivot. Work hard to stay on your course and look for the lessons in every situation.

I am fully committed to making the tough decisions necessary for my growth. I hope you will do the same.

Green Bananas and the story of Kathryn, Nell, and Nathan will help you to remember every time you see green bananas that you need to plan your life. Plan your life, see every day as a special occasion, wave that magic wand, and envision what you want your life to look like. Then, intentionally make decisions and take the necessary actions to make it happen.

I want to leave you with this: I don't care who you are, where you come from, or what your past or current situation may be, it is never too late. You are not too broken. You were born with a purpose, and that purpose is your passion. Today is the first day of the rest of your life. Wave that wand and create the future you want. You are loved by a greater beauty, and I love you.

It is my prayer that you will commit to be the very best version of yourself, and every time you see a green banana, you are reminded to get on track to planning and pursuing your best life.

You're worth it!

GREEN BANANAS

Once upon a time, there were two produce merchants. Nell, who sold fruits and vegetables, always parked her cart next to a butcher, who specialized in small game birds and fish—the smell of which nearly knocked her down from time to time. But she preferred the spot, because it was natural for folks to purchase vegetables and fruits after selecting their protein for the evening meal.

The other merchant, Kathryn, was new. She wasn't interested in selling to the villagers. Her interest was in selling a strange new fruit to other merchants for them to offer to their customers. She was the middleman, employed by a large fruit company, and was just a few sales short of winning salesperson of the month.

Kathryn approached Nell. She admired Nell's selection of veggies and fruits—she even had exotic kiwi and dragon fruits. But when Kathryn showed her a hand of yellow bananas, Nell practically swooned.

"Oh my, what are those?" Nell asked.

"These amazing fruits are called bananas," Kathryn said. "Yellow, ripe bananas. A very sweet fruit." Kathryn peeled a banana and shared it with each of the vendors.

"Delicious." Nell ate the whole banana.

"I'm glad you enjoyed it," Kathryn said with a smile. "They are quite exotic and healthy."

"And so unusual," Nell said. "I'll take three."

Kathryn chuckled. "Do you mean three individual bananas? Or three hands?"

"Hands?" Nell wrinkled her forehead. "That's a funny way to describe them."

"It is, but that's what they call a cluster of bananas, and each individual banana is called a finger."

Nell really laughed at that. "Now, that's so funny. Well, I'll take three, nice hands."

Nell bought all the ripe, yellow bananas Kathryn had on her cart.

"Thank you," Kathryn said. "I'm certain your customers will enjoy them." She was just about to move her cart along when Nell stopped her.

"What is that?" She pointed to a green banana poking out from under a brown tarp on Kathryn's cart.

"Oh," Kathryn said, "they are also bananas, but they're not ripe." She pulled up the tarp. "See, you can't really eat them yet. These green bananas will not be ripe for a couple of days."

Nell looked over the fruit. She looked out over the market and saw that people were starting to gather around her cart, curious about the strange, new, yellow fruit.

"A couple of days?" Nell said. "Uhmm. I'll take them all."

"But they're not ripe," Kathryn said. "I'll come back when they turn yellow."

Nell shook her head. "No, no. I'll purchase them now. This way, when the people finish eating all their ripe bananas, they can come to my cart and purchase more. By then, these green bananas will be ripe."

Kathryn smiled. "So, you don't mind waiting?"

"Let's just say I am good at planning. I know if I wait and plan for the many people coming to my cart in a few days, I will have tremendous sales and be a great success."

The next day, Nell was waiting for Kathryn by the market gates.

Kathryn arrived, pushing her cart that was overflowing with fresh fruits and vegetables—green and yellow bananas.

"Good morning, Kathryn," Nell called. "I see you have more green bananas."

"Sure do," Kathryn said. She pushed her cart into position. "Would you like to purchase more?"

Nell looked over her cart. "Yes. I will take more."

Kathryn shook her head. "I just don't get it. Why would you buy green bananas? Just wait a day or two, and then, you can pick the best ones."

Nell smiled. "I was thinking about this, and I came to the conclusion that you, yourself, are a green banana."

Kathryn took a step back. Her brow wrinkled. "What? Me!"

"No, I mean it," Nell said. "You are a green banana. I'm a green banana. We are all green bananas."

"M-maybe I should peddle my fruit someplace else." She started to push her cart away.

"No, hear me out," Nell said.

Kathryn stopped and turned back. "Okay, tell me. Why are we all green bananas?"

Nell walked out from behind her cart. She invited Kathryn to sit with her on the bench near the pond.

"Come over with me," Nell said. "It's early. The shoppers won't be out for a little while."

Kathryn sat next to Nell. "Feels good to be off my feet. Sometimes, I think I push that cart a hundred miles a day."

"Uhmm, I bet you do. You work hard," Nell said. "You must really like hard work."

Kathryn let go a slight chuckle. "Oh, it pays my bills, but well, I don't know. Sometimes, I wonder what else there is in life."

"Let me ask you a question," Nell said. "If you could wander down to the wizard's shop and purchase a magic wand and wave it in front of you, and POOF, you instantly have the life you want—what would it look like?"

Kathryn laughed at that. "Oh, that's just silly. Magic wands are just props. I could never—"

"Please," Nell said, "just humor me. Close your eyes and imagine what you want for your life."

After a few moments, Kathryn smiled wide. "I would not be

pushing a fruit cart, I can tell you that much. I guess I would want to do much more—a better job, a nice home, a fine horse, nice clothes, and . . . and oh, the list could go on forever."

"See," Nell said. "You are a green banana just waiting to ripen, to become what you were meant to be."

"Oh, I get you now. I guess I *am* a green banana."

The merchants continued to talk for quite a while. Kathryn told Nell all about the life she imagined for herself.

"So, come back tomorrow with your vision, your thoughts on what you want to do with your life," Nell said. "And we'll talk more about it."

That evening, Nell went home to her family. She loved her kids, her spouse, and her dog with all her heart. She wanted nothing more than for them to be happy.

She prepared a nice meal, and the family enjoyed it, as usual. She always had fresh vegetables and fruit to serve her growing children. She had eight!

After dinner, as usual, Nell and the children set about cleaning up the kitchen, while her spouse headed outside to mow the lawn and milk the cows.

Nell was drying a dish when she had a sudden notion. "These dishes are so bland—the same every night, every morning. Just plain, old, white dishes." She put the plate in the cabinet and dashed out of the kitchen.

"Where are you going, Mama?" her oldest asked.

"You'll see. I'll be right back."

Nell climbed into the attic. She quickly located an old steamer trunk and flipped open the lid.

"Ah, there you are." She pulled out the nicest, finest china and silver utensils she had ever seen. They had been a wedding gift many years ago.

"From now on, we are using these dishes and these knives and these forks and these spoons." She looked through the trunk. "And we will sure use these goblets. No more frumperware."

Nell carried the dishes and utensils and goblets into the kitchen. She showed them to her children. "They are so pretty," they said.

"Why haven't we used these before?" asked her oldest daughter.

Nell shook her head. "It sounds silly now, but I was saving them for a special occasion."

"What special occasion?" asked her middle son.

Nell smiled. "That's just it. From now on, every day is a special occasion, and we will use the good stuff. My family deserves the good stuff."

The next morning, after she got the children off to school, Nell pushed her cart back to the market. It was a grand day. The sun was promising to shine bright, and no rain threatened. Nell dressed in her best tunic and striped stockings. She pulled her hair high onto her head and secured it with a pretty comb.

As she pushed her cart down the path toward the market, Nell was surprised that she felt a bit stronger today. She even thought she stood a bit taller and smiled a bit brighter at the people she passed along the way.

Nell pushed her cart into its usual position. She hung her sign up and arranged her wares in order.

William, the fishmonger happened by. "Good morning, Nell," he called. "My, but don't you look nice today."

Nell smiled wide. "Thank you," she called. "And I feel nice also."

A few minutes later, Kathryn arrived. She pushed her fruit cart along the rutted path and stopped at Nell's cart.

Good morning, Kathryn," Nell called.

"Oh, good morning," Kathryn said. But she did not sound at all enthusiastic. "Why are you dressed up?"

"Because it is today," Nell called.

"Today? What's so special about today?"

"I have decided that every day is a special day. So, why not dress for the occasion?"

"But why?" Kathryn looked into the sky. "It looks like clouds are moving in. Your lovely tunic will get all wet and muddy on the walk home."

"No matter," Nell said. "Rain is good to grow our vegetables and fruits."

Kathryn stepped closer to Nell. "I suppose. I wish I had your outlook."

"Why can't you?" Nell peeled a ripe banana. "It's all about—" she bit into the sweet fruit. "It's all about how you think. If you think your life is bad, then it will be. If you think good thoughts, then things can be good."

Kathryn couldn't contain a laugh. "Oh, come on. It is not that simple."

"Look, it's not like just thinking about having a lot of money will get you a lot of money. But thinking positively about how to make a lot of money could, and will, yield great results."

"You think so?"

"I do. This morning, I decided to feel good, to see my life and my work as a positive. I dressed up and put a smile on my face. People noticed. They treated me differently. And I feel terrific."

Kathryn looked toward her shabby sandals. "I guess I could spruce up a bit and think more positively. Maybe it will help."

Nell put her hand on Kathryn's shoulder. "I know it will."

"Did you think about what we discussed yesterday?"

"Yes, yes I did." Kathryn sighed. "I have a vision for my life, and it is nothing like the one I am living now. In my vision, I am successful and enjoying a rich full life with a husband and children, and even a dog or cat or goldfish."

Nell helped a customer.

"I'll take three bunches of carrots, several potatoes, a head of broccoli, and a full pound of those luscious mushrooms."

"Certainly," Nell said. She doled out the goods, and the customer gladly paid, and even offered a compliment. "Such a pretty tunic, Nell. Business must be good."

Nell said thank you and wished her a lovely day.

"Interesting," Nell said. "That customer comes to my stall often, but she usually only buys a few things, one bunch of carrots and perhaps a head of lettuce. But today, she bought plenty."

Nell pulled herself up to her full height. "I think it is because I look nice. I put on my best tunic and brightest striped stockings. I have an air of success. It's contagious."

Kathryn shrugged. "Could be."

"So, tell me," Nell said, "Why do you seem so down in the mouth today?"

"Your little exercise made me quite perplexed. Bothered me."

"Really? How so?" Nell stepped out from behind her cart.

"Well . . . now that I know what I want my life to look like, I am feeling stuck. I have no clue how to make it happen. I mean, my future does not look bright."

"Oh dear, that is a pickle," Nell said.

Once again, Nell invited Kathryn to walk along the pond and chat.

"I'm sorry you feel so down," Nell said. "I didn't mean for that to happen."

"Oh, it's not your fault. I'm just wondering what should I do now? I mean it's great to know what I want my life to look like, but how do I make it happen?"

Nell thought a moment and said, "Well, the first thing is to admit you are a green banana."

Kathryn laughed. "Okay. Okay. My name is Kathryn, and I am a green banana."

"Good." Nell took her friends hands and looked into her eyes. "I know there is so much potential inside you."

"Thanks, but like I said, how do I accomplish anything? I have a business to run and very little money. How do I achieve my goals? I get so discouraged."

Nell added more green stemmed carrots to the carrot bin. "Uhm, there is much to discuss. Let's talk again tomorrow. But for now, do your peddling, and I'll do mine. Meet me in the morning, and we'll talk."

Kathryn looked a bit disappointed. "Okay, Nell. Thanks for listening."

Nell nodded. "It's really my pleasure."

"Perhaps it's time for some big changes," Kathryn said. "Let's see what happens!"

Nell went home that evening, tired but happy. She had sold all her produce and had received quite a few compliments throughout the day. Still, there was a nagging thought in the back of her mind over Kathryn's words about changing her own career.

I had always thought my children were my career, she thought as she opened the garden gate. But they were getting older. The older children could care for the younger ones quite well, and her husband was usually around to help. Could she, herself, consider a career change?

Suppertime came and went, as usual. The children happily reported on their day, while Nell and her husband, Earl, listened intently. After the kitchen was cleaned up by the two oldest children, and after Nell had read the bedtime stories, and after Earl had moved into his hobby room to work on a model sailboat, Nell wandered outside.

The air was chilly. She shivered. "It's cold tonight, but nice." She looked up into the velvet sky and tried to locate Cassiopeia and the Big Dipper. After a few minutes, a star shot across the sky.

"Oh, wow," Nell said. "I love shooting stars. They always seem so . . . so prophetic."

She walked on around her yard. It had been a while since Nell had attended any church services, but this night she was reminded how faith had always played a big role in her life's choices. So, that night, Nell paid heed to that still, small voice in her heart and asked herself, "Should I change my life that much?" Kathryn was correct. Nell did have a gift when it came to listening and offering wisdom. Maybe this should become a career.

The next morning, Nell once again chose to have a clear and happy mindset as she made her way to market. Her cart was full, and so was her heart. Today, she would begin planning to take a new path.

It seemed Kathryn had made a similar decision—although she was not quite as excited as Nell.

"Let's walk," Nell said. "Clouds are rolling in. The market will not be so busy."

Kathryn helped Nell cover her cart. "As I said yesterday, I have no clue where to begin."

They walked on for a few minutes, and then, Nell said, "It would seem to me that the first thing you should do is figure out what is stopping you from achieving what you want for your life."

Nell heard someone ringing the bell on her cart.

"You think a minute, and I'll be right back. I had not expected customers."

Nell was delighted to see a short line gathered in front of her stall. This usually only happened during holidays.

She was quick to wait on each customer as a light rain fell, and she even sold out of most of her fruit—except for a few hands of green bananas.

"I'd rather not have green bananas," the customer said.

"Oh, but if you purchase them today, tomorrow or the next day, they will be perfect. Just at their sweetest."

"Well . . . I suppose," the customer said.

"Excellent." Nell chose the nicest looking bananas and handed them to the customer. "Come back and tell me if it was worth the wait."

"I'll do that," said the customer. "Do I just put them on the table and watch them ripen?"

"Sounds like a good plan," Nell said. Although, since bananas were a new fruit to the villagers, Nell wasn't certain what to do with them.

After all the customers had been taken care of, Nell hurried back to Kathryn.

"I was worried you wouldn't come back," Kathryn said. She was looking out over the pond.

"Oh, no, just a lot of customers."

"That's nice."

They walked on together, not saying much until Kathryn repeated her earlier question. "How do I get to where the magic wand wants to take me?"

"I've been thinking about that," Nell said, "and I think the place to start is to recognize what things are in your way. What are the obstacles?"

Kathryn smiled. "I've never told anyone this, but I want to become a doctor. I think the village could use another doctor. Old Doc Price is not getting any younger."

"That's great," Nell said. "I think you would make a fine doctor. You always know just what to do when there's an emergency. Like the time you took care of Mikey's arm before the doc came."

"I remember. It was broken in two places."

Nell picked a flower. She held it to her nose. "Smells so nice. But winter is coming, and we'll have to prepare for cooler days and longer nights."

"And you," Kathryn said, "are always the one who gets the village prepared for the long winters. And you are always there when someone needs help and counsel."

They walked back to the market square. Kathryn sold more fruits to the vendors, and Nell sold out of nearly all her produce. It was time to close up for the night.

"Why don't you come to my house?" Nell asked Kathryn. "We can talk more about your goals."

"I-I guess I can, thank you."

Kathryn was not married, and she had no children. She usually went home to her empty, little house and ate alone. It had been difficult to make a living all by herself. That didn't make reaching for her goals any easier. It was difficult enough to make a living. How could she ever afford school?

When they arrived at Nell's house, Nell was quick to get her kids started on some chores.

"Wow," Kathryn said, "they seem really eager to do what you tell them. My mother had to threaten us before we got a move on."

Nell poured herself and Kathryn a glass of iced tea. "They know I'm not kidding around. But yeah, they're good kids, and I want them to understand the best way to get what they want—in this case, dinner—is to plan, follow the rules, and do what's required."

"Or they don't eat."

Nell shook her head. "One or two of them have gone without dinner on a rebellious occasion or two."

After dinner, and after Nell's kids and her husband were off doing their own things, Nell got some cookies for Kathryn and herself.

"Come out to the back patio. It's a lovely night. The stars are bright. We can build a little fire in the chimera."

Nell and Kathryn sat across from each other as the flames lapped the night sky.

"How come you did not continue your education? Why did you become a peddler?"

Kathryn shrugged. "Oh, it's a long story."

"We have time," Nell said.

"Well, the long and short of it is my mother died when I was quite young. My father did his best to care for us. I have three siblings." Kathryn rubbed her eye and sniffled. "But he had his problems, and our family fell apart. I left home the minute I could."

Nell hugged Kathryn. "I'm so sorry that happened," she said as she patted Kathryn's back.

"Thank you," Kathryn said. "You can see how impossible it is for me to do anything more to achieve my magic wand life."

Nell pulled away. "Nonsense. You can do it. I have learned that people do what they want. And if you want to become a doctor—then do it."

"Seriously?" Kathryn said. "But . . . but how?"

"I think you need to make a plan," Nell said. "But first, you have to decide if you really and truly want to become a doctor."

"I do," Kathryn said with a bit of triumph in her voice. "I absolutely do."

"Terrific," Nell said. "So, start to plan."

"Plan? I don't even know where to begin."

"I would first check out the schools," Nell said. "Ask about classes, tuition—all that stuff. Figure out how to make it all work

while still peddling your bananas—and other fruits."

"Sounds like a lot," Kathryn said.

Nell gazed into the flames.

"It *is* a lot. It's not going to be easy. But you can make it

work."

Kathryn shook her head.

"Uhmm." Nell rested her hand on her friend's arm. "You

just said you were sure. But now, you sound doubtful. Are you sure

you want to be a doctor? Because right now, you seem to be making

excuses. You'll never get there if you don't start somewhere."

"No," Kathryn said. "I am sure."

"Really sure?" Nell said.

Kathryn nodded and smiled. "I am."

Nell added wood to the fire. "I think you need a vision board."

Kathryn chuckled. "What is that?"

"Write out what you want. Find pictures of doctors or colleges

or books or . . . doctor tools, anything that will remind you of your

goal. Paste them on a board and put it in a place where you will see it

every day."

"Okay, Nell, if you say so. Then what?"

"You do what we just said. Go to school."

"Will you go down to the school with me?"

"Of course. I want to check out some courses for myself

anyway."

Nell and Kathryn headed to the college the next day. The village university was just on the outskirts of town, so they were able to walk. It was such a nice day, although there was talk of rain moving in a little later.

"I'm a little nervous," Kathryn said.

"Of course, you are," Nell said. "This is a whole new adventure for you. But you must be thrilled, too."

Kathryn plucked a leaf from a tree. "Yes, of course, but there are so many unknowns. Can I really handle the classes? What about tuition? Books? Will I be able to look after my business?"

"Your bananas will be fine," Nell laughed.

A couple of hours later, Nell and Kathryn were headed home. Kathryn carried an armful of pamphlets and books and papers. She was all set to begin school the next semester, which started in just a couple of weeks.

On the walk home, they bumped into Nathan Tuck. He was not a very nice man, often chased kids away, and could rarely find the good in anything.

Kathryn accidentally stepped on his property as they passed.

"Hey, get off my lawn!" Tuck called. "I work hard on that."

Kathryn was so startled, she spun round quickly and dropped her papers and books on Nathan's grass.

Tuck hollered, "Get off my lawn. Now look what you did."

"Just ignore him," Nell said. "Let's get your stuff picked up."

Dark clouds rolled over head, and thunder boomed in the distance. A swift wind kicked up and blew some of Kathryn's papers across Nathan's lawn.

He dashed off his porch and snatched them up.

"Hey," Kathryn called. "I need those, Mr. Tuck. Please."

"What are they?" he asked.

"For school. I'm starting college and…"

"College?" You? Ah you're nothing but a fruit peddler. You'll never make it." He laughed.

Kathryn looked down. "I need those papers," she whispered.

"So, go get them," Nell said.

"I-I can't. He frightens me, and maybe he's right. I am just a fruit peddler."

Nell shook her head. "If you truly believe that, then yes, you will never succeed. But I don't believe it for one second."

Kathryn looked up. "Please, Mr. Tuck. May I have my papers back?"

"Louder," Nell said. "Make sure he hears you. Stand up for yourself and your dreams."

"Look, Mr. Tuck," Kathryn called, "you can't keep those. They belong to me. Now you need to hand them over."

"They were on my property." Nathan Tuck let go a wicked laugh.

Kathryn backed away. "I'll try again later."

"No," Nell said as rain pelted the ground.

"And look," Kathryn said, "my first textbook over there. It's getting all muddy."

"Go get it," Nell said. She gave her friend a little push.

Kathryn sucked in a deep breath as she looked Nell square in the eye. "I'm going." She marched onto Tuck's lawn and grabbed her textbook. She wiped the water and dirt off and tucked it under her apron. "Now please, Mr. Tuck, I need those papers."

Tuck just continued to laugh.

Nell took Kathryn's hand. "Someone once said, when life gives you lemons you make lemonade."

"What?" Kathryn said.

"Find a solution. Find another way. Make something good out of a sour situation."

Kathryn pulled herself up. "You know what? I'm sure the school will give me new papers. I don't need Mr. Tuck." She looked at the crotchety old man on the porch who clutched her papers like they were treasure. She chose another route. "Go on, keep them. I'll just go back to the university and get copies."

Then, she stomped off Mr. Tuck's lawn in a huff.

"I'm proud of you," Nell said when they were out of sight of Mr. Tuck.

Kathryn looked at Nell with wide eyes. The rain poured down. "That was . . . exhilarating."

"Standing up for yourself—making wise choices—often is."

When they reached Kathryn's home, Nell found a stick. She drew two, giant check marks in the mud.

"What's that?" Kathryn asked.

"Check. You just hurdled two huge hurdles. You are on your way now."

Kathryn nodded. "Listen Nell, thanks for helping me. You're a good friend."

"My pleasure. I enjoy watching people become their true authentic selves and achieve their goals."

"Well, I sure am grateful for you."

Nell hugged Kathryn. "Well thanks, but don't forget to be grateful for yourself. I always find that being grateful for the things I have—family, friends, the stars up above, a cool rain. All that helps me be successful. There is something about positivity that brings about good things."

"Well, I'm gonna stay positive and grateful and…"

"Get to work."

Kathryn smiled wide. "Who would ever thought that some green bananas would have turned into something like this?"

A few weeks passed, and Kathryn was busy in school. She didn't have as much time to take long walks with Nell. Nell missed her friend, but she also felt quite good that Kathryn was off pursuing her dreams.

One day, the old curmudgeon, Nathan Tuck showed up at the market. He was quite amused by Nell's basket of green bananas. He laughed and pointed at them. "That's the most ridiculous fruit I have ever seen."

It didn't take long for a small crowd to gather.

"No, no," said a person in the crowd. "They're delicious. Just have to wait for them to turn yellow."

Many in the crowd cheered for the new fruit.

"Oh pish," Tuck said. "I haven't time to wait for fruit. I like my fruit ripe when I purchase it. This is preposterous."

"But, Mr. Tuck," Nell said, "I know if you just tried it, you wouldn't be disappointed."

The crowd urged the old man on.

Finally, he bought three green bananas.

"You know what?" Nell said as she handed Tuck the fruit. "You are a green banana."

Tuck jumped back. "What in the blazes? How dare you speak to me like that!"

"It's not an insult," Nell said. "Those bananas have great potential, and so do you, I think."

"Nonsense," Tuck said. And he walked away.

The villagers continued to talk about the old man after he had disappeared down the lane. But Nell felt kind of sad for him. She thought that surely, there went a man who probably had never reached his potential, who had never reached for the stars or thought about his goals.

The next day, Nell decided to visit Nathan Tuck. She knew he could very well just throw her off his property, but one thing about Nell was she never had a problem taking big risks. The payoff was usually well worth the effort.

Nell stood out front of Tuck's house waiting for him to come outside. She waited several minutes, but then took another bold move. She opened the gate and walked right up to his front door. She knocked.

"Who's there?'

"It's Nell, from the market. I brought you some more green bananas and a couple yellow ones."

The door swung open.

"You did, eh. Well, take them away. The ones you sold me yesterday are still green."

"Growth takes time, Nathan."

It took a few moments, but Nathan finally walked toward Nell to take the bananas.

Much to her surprise and delight, Nathan Tuck allowed Nell to tell him about her passion for helping people be the best they can and reach their full potential.

"Potential?" Nathan scoffed. "I was just a workin' man my whole life. Worked hard at a job I hated."

As they talked, Nell discovered some very surprising truths

about Nathan Tuck. He even brought her inside and showed her his artwork. He was quite talented at taking scraps of metal and welding them into spectacular designs—clocks, gates, sculptures of animals, and even a spectacular bookcase.

"You do woodworking as well?" Nell asked.

Nathan looked away for a moment, and then said, "Well, y-yes. My father taught me."

"You should turn this into a business," Nell told him. "Tell the world about your art and your abilities. People will buy this stuff."

"Aww, but this place is so small. I would need a larger studio—a place I can really spread out. Just never had the gumption to move, though."

"I think you should," Nell said. "You should find the place that's right for you—big enough for you to make amazing works of art and have a business."

"Mayhaps," Nathan said.

Nell looked at the clock on Nathan's wall. "I must be getting home."

As they stood on the porch, Nathan cracked what Nell thought might be his first smile in ages. Then, he chuckled. "I haven't smiled since before Lotabell, my wife, passed."

Nell nodded. "So, now is the perfect time to change your environment and reach for the stars. Dream a little… or a lot."

Nell turned to leave.

"One thing," Nathan called. "Tell that other woman you were with the other day—tell her I'm sorry, and I hope she does well in school."

"She could be your doctor one day."

Nathan slapped his knee. "Guess I better watch out then."

The next day, Nathan went to the market, where he told everyone about the delicious bananas. "Just had to give 'em some time. But they sure are tasty now."

Snow came early to the village, and Nell, like the other vendors, was forced to close her stall for the season. But as she parked her cart near her house and covered it with a large, yellow tarp, she smiled. "It's going to be fine."

The family dog scurried up to her. She sat on her haunches and raised a paw to Nell. "I know, girl. We've got this. I will use this as an opportunity to start my new business."

Nathan even made a beautiful sign for Nell—*The Mentor is In,* which she proudly accepted and hung on her door.

After some studying and soul-searching—and a lot of leaning on faith—Nell decided it was time to turn her passion for helping others into a business. She already had a few clients, including Nathan Tuck, and of course, Kathryn. She wouldn't charge Kathryn for her services. There was joy in pro bono work as well.

After a few days, Nell had her office all set up. Kathryn was her first client.

"I'm doing well," Kathryn said. "Classes are good, the teachers are very interesting, and my grades are excellent."

"I knew you could do it."

As they talked, Kathryn noticed another sign on Nell's office wall:

RAMS

"Rams?" Kathryn said. "What is that?"

Nell explained what the four letters stood for.

"Oh, that's an acrostic I came up with to help us remember some important points about reaching your dreams."

Kathryn smiled.

"'R' for relevant," Nell said. "Your chosen profession and personal goals should align with your values. They should be 'A', attainable, for when you know what you most desire, you will find a way to make it happen."

"Oh, that makes sense. What does the 'M' stand for?"

"Measurable, to measure your progress. Doing this will help you keep you motivated. And the 'S' means 'specific'. What do you plan to do or be? Your goal should be clear and include a due date."

"I guess becoming a doctor is pretty specific."

"Yes," Nell said, "and I believe your goal fits all the criteria."

Relevant
Attainable
Measurable
Specific

Months later, Nell's counseling services became a thriving business. She had made a dream come true and was enjoying her life. Nathan Tuck had his first art show and sold several pieces. He wasn't quite so mean anymore. He had stopped making excuses. Nell told him that he could have either excuses or results, but he could not have both. He had, for the most part, put his stinking thinking behind him. And at Nell's urging, Nathan made a goal to do one kind thing for another person every week. He didn't tell her when one kind thing became three kind things. He enjoyed the feeling that came along with the good deeds.

Kathryn was well on her way to becoming a doctor. She visited with Nell as often as she could. She had built her vision board,

which brought her motivation and joy. Some of the pictures and words changed as she met certain goals. Nell had taught her to make new goals when old ones were met. Always reach for the next level. Kathryn decided to forgive her father, another important step on the road to becoming a ripe banana. Forgiveness made it possible for Kathryn to move forward with joy.

Nell went on to become the most popular friend in the village, always ending every conversation with the same thought, "I hope you have the best day and best life possible. You are worth it!"

Tina Holt moves audiences everywhere with the message of Green Bananas. She is a managing broker in the real estate industry, serving the coastal regions of Virginia, North Carolina and Maryland and much sought after Leadership and Life Coach. She is the proud mother of three servicemen and Mimi to five grandchildren. She lives to see each and every person reach their highest potential.

CPSIA information can be obtained
at www.ICGtesting.com
Printed in the USA
BVHW090958170920
588927BV00031B/942